18 Holes with Belichick and Brady

BENJAMIN PLAUT

DEDICATION

To my mother Sharon, who read to my
sisters and me when we were little.

CONTENTS

ACKNOWLEDGMENTS

Thank you to Dave Rundell, Kelly Fordyce, John Taylor, Roger Rundell, Ben Mouton, John DeMarchi, and Martin Plaut, each of whom read this in different drafts and gave notes; and to my friends from Brown –including those I played football with as a senior– who ask me at every reunion and get together when I will start publishing.

First edition cover photo: Kelly Fordyce

First edition author photo: Jordan Ancel

INTRODUCTION

In February 2012, Bill Belichick and Nick Saban were paired in the same group for the PGA Tour's Pebble Beach Pro-Am. I had planned to drive up from Los Angeles to walk the round watching the two coaches on the one day that fit my schedule. The weather forecast was bad, so I decided against driving the ten hours combined in case the round was washed out. It wasn't. I decided if I ever got another chance to see them, I would go.

Two years later, Belichick was paired with Tom Brady.

1. GETTING THERE

February 2014. The forecast called for cool temperatures and drizzle, with heavier rains and wind ahead.

It meant the galleries might be small, but that it also might be miserable out there. Right on the ocean. Northern California.

I drove up the coast from Los Angeles at night and stayed in a motel I found online for fifty dollars, 25 miles from the event.

I woke up very early, parked at Pebble Beach, and took a shuttle to the course Belichick and Brady were playing.

The event uses three courses. For their

Friday round Belichick and Brady would be playing the Monterey Peninsula Country Club's Shore Course.

The shuttles dropped you somewhere on the course well away from the practice area and first tee. It was about an hour before their tee time, and Brady and Belichick would be teeing off on the tenth hole.

I asked a man and a woman in a golf cart, staff or volunteers, where the driving range and putting green were.

"Far away," they said. They offered me a ride.

I hopped on the back, standing.

I wore black running pants, a performance running shirt under a lightweight black pullover and a light black zip-up jacket. I wore soft-spike golf shoes and a dark blue baseball cap with a simple white hotel logo on it. It was what I wore a lot, except for the golf shoes. Wearing what I wore a lot, I looked like a PGA Tour player.

"It's a 35 to 40-minute walk to get back here if they are teeing off on ten," said the guy in the cart. He then turned around and drove.

Yeah sure, 35-40 minutes if you knew the route and didn't get held up by ropes and galleries and waits for people to putt out or tee off. It could be an hour.

I would miss the first few holes for a chance to see the warm up.

Maybe I'd find another friendly cart out of nowhere.

2. THE DRIVING RANGE

I get dropped off at the driving range, which is pretty much empty. The far end is completely empty. In the middle there are three pros, including Graeme McDowell, with an audience of six. Thirty yards closer to me, alone with his caddie on this end, is Tom Brady.

I walk over, stand directly behind them, and watch Brady warm up. He hits the ball pretty well and with some real length.

He lived in Boston, just finished a professional football season a couple weeks prior, and probably had not touched a club from July until this first week in February. His warm-up looked like any other good golfer working on something to take out on the course after an extended layoff.

Brady used his caddie as a teaching professional a little, exchanging a few words here and there, always about the set-up or swing. At one point he worked on a specific footwork issue with the caddie as a pro for a few real swings in a row, but mostly he was trying to groove something he could use.

Brady mostly hit woods. He may have hit irons before I got there.

No one else watched.

Thirty minutes.

One couple that watched the pros for a few minutes came by for a minute but no more, acknowledging who he was and going on their way.

Just me, Tom Brady, and his caddie for half an hour.

Worth the trip.

3. THE PRACTICE GREEN

Brady goes over to chip. I walk over to the putting green/chipping area.

Belichick is there and they greet and shake hands. Warmly, but as you might meet a boss or coach you like.

"Hey, good to see you."

Belichick has a Wesleyan buddy on the bag and is moving from the chipping area to the putting green. Brady chips. Wayne Gretzky, Kid Rock, Darius "Hootie" Rucker, and a couple pros are on the putting green. There are maybe a dozen people watching. Fewer for much of it.

One couple has a young son, who is wearing a New England Patriots jersey and quietly holding a football as he watches. At some point, unprompted by anything other than the sight of the small boy in the jersey with the football, Belichick comes over from the putting green and signs it.

"You want Tom's, too?" he asks.

The child nods silently, but clearly.

Belichick walks over to the chipping area carrying the football –maybe thirty yards– has a brief conversation with Brady, and Brady signs.

Five or six minutes later, as Brady is done with his chipping and just getting settled on the putting green… another young kid with another football, another unprompted Belichick signature, another "volunteer" by Belichick of the Brady bonus. Another walk for Belichick with a football. Another pause for Brady to sign.

Brady can putt, and his chipping looked decent. Six months of no golf and a big event and stage as a test.

He was wearing old gray pants with a hole or tear in them and, like me, a black turtleneck or black high-necked pullover, light black zip-up jacket, and dark blue baseball cap with a simple white logo on it – albeit his own.

It was time to go to the tenth tee where they were starting.

Even if I would miss two or three holes getting over to the back nine to catch up with them, it had been cool at the practice area.

4. "I'M NOT PLAYING. BUT YEAH."

I walk over to player shuttles and ask if Group 19 has left already.

"Yes, just did."

I wince.

The man reads my face.

"Are you supposed to be with them?"

"Yeah."

I wasn't Brady or Belichick, and one pro was fairly well known, so I had to be the other pro or some coach or friend or somebody.

I look legit. I look like an athlete. I am an athlete, a month away from a fifth straight L.A. Marathon. I had spent the last nine years in Hollywood, sometimes at the hottest nightclubs or restaurants, sometimes on sets, stages, and red carpets. I am legit.

I just want a ride. I had ridden over *standing on the back of a golf cart.* There is a line of cars with drivers just sitting there— more cars than there are people on the putting green and practice area combined.

He looks at me. He looks at the list. He looks at me.

"I'm not playing. But yeah."

He puts me in a waiting, running car,

and I sit in the back seat silently as the driver
begins to drive.

My ride, longer than imagined, makes
me thankful I did not have to walk. We go
through real streets and neighborhoods
minute after minute, a few miles. I would
have missed holes and maybe taken
inefficient paths to get there. There is one
other car in the drop zone as we arrive, and
the driver parks right behind the other
vehicle. The drop zone is on the ocean side
of the road, a small patch of gravel next to the
rocks leading down to the water.

I thank the driver, step out, and start to
walk toward the path up toward the course.
Belichick steps out of the other vehicle. He
looks at me for a moment to greet me as if I

am the pro, pauses a second, and I walk on and look ahead.

We walk through the ropes together, three or four yards apart. We walk across the fairway. It is gray by the water, the Pacific coast. There is no one around. And I am walking across the fairway with Belichick.

We get to the next ropes, through those and to yet another set of ropes, this one with fans who want him to sign stuff, which, headed straight to the tee, he cannot. As he goes on to the tee, I slide into the small gallery. He goes back with Brady to meet with their pros on the back tees. The amateurs tee off from the white tees, but on many holes they wait with their pros on the back tees, then all walk to the whites.

In the Pro-Am, the amateurs each play with a pro, the amateur with their handicap strokes on the hole if any, and the best score of the two counts each hole. For golf purposes, Brady and Belichick are amateurs.

The tenth hole, their first, has a long distance back uphill to the back tees – and the path to the back tees is roped off.

5. WAYNE GRETZKY, KID ROCK, AND JOHN DALY

I go to the white tees. There are seven or eight people there including two in Patriots jerseys.

Also on the white tees, four feet away, are Wayne Gretzky and Kid Rock.

They are playing with John Daly, who is wearing American flag pants way back on the back elevated tee no one can see well.

Their pros tee off.

Now it is Gretzky's turn. He has a cigar. He is wearing the uniform of the day, dark running/golf/rain gear. He decides not to wait for the pros, nor the lady who whispered the intro to the pros from the back roped off tee no one could get near or hear her from. The pros and the lady have not even started off the tee down the hill.

Gretzky looks around slowly at the eight of us with his tee, ball, club and cigar in his hands and says,

"From Brantford, Ontario... Wayne Gretzky."

I laugh and clap. Six of the eight people clap, half laugh.

The greatest hockey player of my lifetime, so cool on and off the ice, telling an inside joke with full eye contact the whole way.

And, on this rare day, Wayne Gretzky is just the opening act I will basically ignore from now on as I follow Brady and Belichick.

6. BRADY AND BELICHICK TEE OFF

After a wait and once Gretzky, Rock, Daly, and Gretzky's pro partner Dustin Johnson have cleared the fairway, Belichick and Brady's pros hit from the back tees. Brady and Belichick come into view, walking down the path toward the tee.   Where there were eight people for Gretzky and Kid Rock, less than ten minutes later there are now close to 25 people, a good number of them with Pats jerseys and stuff to sign.

Since their pros have hit, Brady and Belichick must get set and tee off fairly efficiently, and both ignore the well-wishers. One guy yells out that he is a friend of a friend some name to Brady.   Brady completely ignores him the first time.   He yells again. Brady, without looking away from his target in the fairway says, "Tell him I say hello," with a tone and the universally understood unstated follow: *Now be quiet so I can hit,* and goes back to ignoring him.

Brady is in the fairway on ten, our first hole, a Par 5, and hits his second shot further down the fairway, leaving him with a long wedge or 9-iron to an uphill green about 130 to 140 yards out. By the time I get to his shots, half of the throng on the tee is gone and not following. There will be a dozen tops following this group early.

I am walking around a golf course by the Northern California ocean. I am in perfect position to watch Brady's third shot and see the green where it may land.

An attractive older woman stops next to me. She and a big man move on forward a bit before the shot.

Brady hits his third shot to fourteen feet for a natural birdie possibility on one.

Belichick's fourth shot, a chip, leaves him with a putt for par.

Brady makes natural birdie on one.

7. HALL OF FAME SHOES

On our second hole (the eleventh), the attractive older woman comes up and stands next to me again as I am first to the spot from where I want to view Brady's shot. The big man lumbers ahead 40 yards with his mini-chair which he sits on.

I watch Brady's shot with the woman.

Eventually we are all walking up the hill. She and the man begin walking ahead of me, and they are probably 65-70 years old, although she looks good and is upright and strong. He is a big man. At times walking uphill with some sort of injury or pain, labored, like a former football player or basketball player, but he is determined and moving forward, usually positioning himself ahead of the small crowd on a carry foldout chair.

He is walking in front of me now. I watch his gait on the wet slick uphill slightly muddy climb, in part for my own protection. I notice he is wearing Patriots sneakers, and then I see they are Super Bowl game sneakers, with a TB 12 in faded Sharpie. He is wearing Hall of Fame shoes climbing the wet path through the grass. These are Brady's parents.

Now knowing who they are, I try not to stand near them; but on three in the fairway, Mrs. Brady comes over and stands right next to me with no one around. Mr. Brady stands next to her. We watch Tom at his ball, but there is a longer wait than usual. It is another Par 5. The group ahead is not yet on the green.

Tom walks over. This is his first chance to say hello to his parents all day, and I do not need to crash this party.

There is no one within fifty yards as he walks over. I am within a foot or two of his mom, her positioning, and I decide to politely step away, enough to be out of earshot and give them room, but still close enough to see the next shot. As I do so, Brady looks at me and acknowledges my gesture, silently, but with a slight, real nod of acknowledgment, like, thanks.

Eventually a small group of fans from

back on the tee –seven people, two in Patriots jerseys– apparently motivated by seeing Brady at the rope, catch up to us. After a brief pause at the 15-18 foot perimeter example I have modeled, two fans then four of the fans crowd the Bradys for autographs. One, a girl with a Massachusetts accent and a few drinks under her belt by 10:30 a.m., offers Brady a can of beer. He declines. He tells his parents he will talk to them later and walks back to his shot. These fans do not follow the group for long.

Mrs. Brady joins me wherever I stop. Sometimes Mr. Brady goes ahead and puts his chair so he is part way to the next stop.

It will be a six or seven mile walk on moist turf in February weather.

8. PROUD MOM

I have a Ziploc bag of goodies. It is cold and gray. I pull out the bag: pretzel rods broken into halves, Pep-O-Mint Life Savers, sugarless gum, and Pine Bros cough drops. I open it and offer some to Mrs. Brady. She takes a pretzel and says thank you and smiles.

Her name is Galynn. We start talking. Some people over the course of our first nine holes say hello or talk to Tommy's dad, Tom. Tom Sr., his father, is "Tom"; "Tommy" is her son, the quarterback.

I tell her about me, my upcoming move from L.A. to Houston. How I really started studying the greatness of Brady and Belichick once Bill O'Brien got hired—that I knew OB at Brown, and played football my senior year, though most of it on scout team.

She tells me about her kids, including her nurse daughter in Santa Monica. She talks of her kids with the pride of great parents. There are grandkids, too. I am sure the sisters are impressive. You can see from the parents where the children get their start.

"You'll have two kids in L.A. now," I say, wistful about the fact that I am leaving Los Angeles in months. One more marathon in March, then the process of setting up practice in Houston.

"Tommy and Giselle are going to sell that house, so just one."

This was news. It was also a cool mom talking about her grown kids, each with equal interest and love, each with pride.

People do go up and talk to Tom Sr. He talks with them briefly. But, for the most part it is me and Galynn. Sometimes, I stop to watch Belichick up close while Galynn positions herself to see Tommy better.

The Bradys and I usually separate somewhere near the putting green. They maneuver ahead to see Tommy closer. I usually stop in the best place to watch all the putting.

9. BELICHICK'S GAME

There are times, if the shot is more easily viewed, where I can watch how Belichick approaches his challenges. He is focused. He grinds. He follows through on his full swings.

Belichick is one of the older amateurs in the field and is maybe a 14-16 handicap with a fairly steady game. Lots of bogeys but fighting for par every hole. And he probably hadn't touched a club since July either.

He hits the ball with average-plus length for someone his age, but from the same tees that Brady is playing from, and in cool, wet conditions, the par fours can be long for him.

Belichick follows through to the target well when finishing his putts, especially for his handicap.

On this day at least, Belichick's putting looks to be the strength of his game.

10. LUNCH WITH THE BRADYS AND LINDA HOLLIDAY

Linda Holliday joins us somewhere in the middle-end of the first nine, which today is the back nine. She is Belichick's girlfriend, his significant other for years.

Galynn introduces us.

The next time we stop, Linda asks,

"How long have you known them?"

"Since today."

Linda seems momentarily taken aback, and then relaxes. Galynn likes me and has vouched for me, including telling her I know Bill O'Brien. I seem cool. They both talk with me as we walk for another hour. Usually Galynn and I walk together, sometimes Linda and I walk together if Galynn is with Tom.

If Belichick comes over to Linda, and no one else is around, I step away. They are affectionate. When either of the players walk over to their families, I give them room. Otherwise, Gaylnn, Linda, and sometimes Tom, Sr. usually walk with me along the ropes.

Eventually, the Ziploc bag is not enough. Galynn has expanded beyond pretzels and the two of us have done the bag some damage.

On the third or fourth hole of the course, the twelfth or thirteenth of the round starting on the back for us, there is a small snack shack with several people in line and tables. Everyone is hungry. Food seems like a really good idea. We have been walking in the cool mist for three hours by the ocean after whatever time it took us to get to the course. Plus, I spent an hour at the range and practice area.

Tom Sr, Galynn, Linda, and I walk ahead to the mid-hole snack shack before the group tees off, and we all wait briefly in line together. We order hot dogs and chips from a very limited menu (essentially hot dogs and chips) and I get water and some of them get Cokes, and we stand or sit (I can't remember if there were chairs) at a portable white picnic table, and we eat and talk. I am the newcomer, so they ask about me a lot and seem interested in me. I talk while we eat. At one point, Galynn wipes mustard from the corner of my lip. It is effortless and natural.

Then for a moment, I am embarrassed. Galynn handled it so perfectly and everyone rolled with it, but still. I said some sort of apology, which they all immediately waved off, Tom Sr. greeting it with, "It's mustard on a hot dog. It happens to everybody." He then wiped his mouth in a show of solidarity or universality.

Belichick and Brady are already on the next tee, and we are done eating, so we go back to walking the course.

11. MARATHON TRAINING AND LOS ANGELES

Linda, when she walks with me, talks about half-marathon training. She is training for her first half-marathon. Bill, who has run marathons in the past, will join her in the spring to run the Nashville Half.

I have 14 miles of hills the next day, then 22 miles the Saturday after. Then, finally, a taper for my race, my fifth L.A. Marathon in a row.

At some point, I tell Linda how impressed I am with Bill and Tom(my). Consistent excellence in a league designed to prevent that, the way they do things, especially the way they stay on message. I tell her I listen to their press conferences and their weekly radio appearances off the team website. I tell her I try to use them as models on how to do it.

She agrees with their greatness. She is impressed by how well they work together.

We talk about her life and family, her daughters who are testing out Los Angeles.

I give my nine years of Los Angeles insight and warnings in small simple doses. Some of it was neighborhood specific, but the basics are obvious. It's expensive. Housing is very expensive. Every work opening is competitive. Anything involving creative arts or fame is even more competitive. Traffic is insane. Parking is an issue. Even if you do earn, taxes are very high. Everyone who is already there is not giving up ground willingly. Distractions are everywhere, and there are plenty of dangerous people. You are competing against the movie stars, rich kids, best locals, plus some of the best from everywhere else in the world, and money matters. The weather is perfect, of course, and anything you want to do is available... if you can make it through traffic to get there.

Mostly we talk about her half-marathon training. After five years of marathon running –each with six months of training with some excellent athletes– I am doing my best coaching, going over the checklist for what to bring on race day, then dealing with the pre-race time in the corral.

On that one issue, she cuts me short.

"We get an escort."

Oh, right, well… then I go into warm-ups with that in mind. But we talk about training: I tell her to mix in hills, especially if there are hills on the course. We talk about everything from nutrition, hydration, sunscreen, to using Body Glide to prevent chafing. We talk about running in whatever weather and running long at the time of the race each week to get the body ready and to learn what works and does not for nutrition and hydration on long runs so one knows what to eat for breakfast and what to eat the night before. We talk about race preparation down to playlists on headphones.

She does more treadmill work, she says.

I say I lived in L.A. so I didn't have to.

I didn't tell her the L.A. outdoor running details. I could run from my front door on the Hollywood/West Hollywood line to the top of Runyon Canyon and back as a 5-miler with hills, six-plus if I ran to the back gate where the house with the horses was. I could train by the water (the Venice/Santa Monica strand and the path through Palisades Park) with my run group. I could run the hills around Dodger Stadium. I could run on the track at Drake Stadium at UCLA, which was a great place to run, especially in the evenings, if you didn't want to have to think about vehicle traffic and didn't mind running lap after lap. Plus Drake was a great place to do speed work.

Instead, I recommend some real road work approaching the race but tell her all miles better than none.

12. TOM BRADY ASKS MY ADVICE IN AN ATHLETIC EVENT

Belichick and Brady do not talk to each other, except the occasional "Nice putt," or "Nice shot." They are with their caddies, and also watching their pro partners. They are playing their own games.

Only once do they talk. On some tee like 1 or 2 (which was our 10th or 11th) where there was a 40-stair climb down from the blues to the whites, Belichick and Brady go down to the whites, where there was a bench behind the white tees on the side away from the ropes. They sit far away enough to be alone with a wall of nature behind them leading up to the back tee. They sit and talk for seven minutes. Two others and I watch the whole time though we can hear nothing.

The best coach and the best quarterback, just talking, waiting for the group in front of them to clear.

On their 14th or 15th hole, the fifth or sixth on the course, Brady is in the right rough behind a split tree that looked like a V with a giant bush (a yard or two after the tree) blocking any shot that would go through the split tree. He can punch out left into the fairway maybe 10 yards, gamble left going super low under a no-chance overhang, or bail way right going low under the split on the right side of the V –under the right tree branch– where there should be out of bounds, but are only backyards with no markers.

There are nine people around me now, maybe ten.

Brady looks back right at me. I have watched him all day since the range. He knows this. I am cool with his parents. He knows this, too. He looks at me.

"What do you think?"

I pause for a second. Tom Brady is asking me what to do in an athletic event. He should hit a low-right push shot. But it takes me a moment to figure out how to positively phrase a message of "bail out" to Tom Brady. I come up with the words: "There is room on the right," but as I open my mouth to say it...

"You got this. Tight windows," says some guy to my left.

That single second freeze –because I

did not expect to be asked– and how can you tell Tom Brady to bail out, to hit a low right bailout and hope you don't hit a house? That there's no out of bounds on the right. That you still have to get it under the right overhang, which is a little higher and roomier than the left. And you still have to not hit a house, unless you are using someone's house as a Green Monster outfield wall since there is no out of bounds on this hole right.

Brady has heard what he needs from tight windows guy. He turns to his shot. I say nothing.

He lines up for a push and hits a low, 175-yard punch four or five-iron right –the *perfect* low-right push shot– which winds up on someone's lawn near their back door, a wedge from the green. The four residents of the home are all in their backyard as spectators. Two of them are wearing Patriots gear. One a Brady jersey.

Imagine that. Bail out into a perfect lie in a backyard with no out of bounds and your fans live there.

There hasn't been anyone on a lawn *all day*. These people, Brady's fans, have his ball land *in their backyard where they are standing*. Since it is their property, and in play, they stand nearer to him than most would. And, since it is their lawn, they grab a quick photo with Brady after the shot. [In 2014 cameras and mobile phones were not allowed at PGA Tour events.] He then hustles up to the green in a striding jog.

Brady keeps playing well. He is good at golf. He is probably a mid-single digit handicap, or could be with even minimal practice.

On 16 (7 by course number) the players are far away from the ropes—a par three green away from everyone. I talk some more with Linda then.

13. BELICHICK: "WELL, I'VE HAD THAT SHOT ALL DAY."

On their 17th hole, the 8th hole on the course, Belichick hits his approach shot in the right rough just by the ropes. I am feet away. No one else is around. He hits a great out from heavy, damp rough 55 yards to a thin slice of elevated, elements-exposed green: pin high, 15 feet from the hole.

"Nice shot," I say.

"Well," he says looking at me, "I've had that shot all day."

Minutes later, he barely misses the par save and is visibly disappointed, a missed opportunity for a net birdie to help his team.

14. GOODBYES

As we walk toward the final tee, it is clear the day is coming to an end. Both Galynn and Linda had asked on separate occasions early on if I would be back again on Saturday. No, I had to run. Now, they ask again. No, heading back to L.A. tonight to run with the run group tomorrow morning at dawn. This would be it, one really cool day.

There are shuttles there at the 9th tee, their 18th, a Par 3. The weather is getting worse. There is a back-up at the tee. The 9th green has no way to walk near it as a spectator. You basically have to skip to ten, which they have already played. This will be it.

Belichick comes over to Linda and acknowledges me. We shake hands.

I introduce myself, then, "Good luck in the Nashville Half."

Belichick pauses for a beat, the distant Nashville Half Marathon not on his radar screen heading to the 18th tee at the Pebble Beach Pro-Am.

He then smiles and half laughs, "Thanks."

I step away.

They hit their shots. Linda slips under the ropes and walks the hole with Bill, the lone patron to do so all day.

Galynn and I walk toward the shuttles. Someone is there to pick up the Bradys in a car. She thanks me for a nice day and so nice to meet you.

She says she wishes there was some way –and then pauses– and explains that she can't invite me to dinner because they really all have to meet back at the hotel to figure things out and usually, since they so rarely have Tommy in town, they like to be just family anyway, but it would have been nice, and it was so nice to meet you.

I thanked her, told her I did not expect a dinner invitation, had a wonderful day enjoying the round and lunch with them, and thanks.

15. HEADING HOME

By the time I took the shuttle to the parking lot and got on the road, it was dark and late and I was really hungry. I ate a pizza and salad at some brick oven place, filled the tank and headed south.

I woke up early the next morning and ran the 14 miles of hills around Dodger Stadium well with the run group. I ran the 22 miles well the next week.

I ran the March 9, 2014 L.A. Marathon well in 4:08:33, a top 15% finish at a 9:29 mile/pace. At age 45 it was my personal best.

ABOUT THE AUTHOR

Benjamin Plaut played golf and football at Brown University. He was a sports writer and columnist for *The Brown Daily Herald*. He became an attorney in 1994. This is his first book.

90093154R00036